Sparks of insight

Anthology of Essays

Students Insights of
Al-Ameer English School, Ajman

DECANIMPRINT
Think Globally

English Language
Sparks of Insight
(Articles)
Compiled by
Al-Ameer English School, Ajman

Published in November 2023
by Decan Imprint Publishing Co.
Reg. Off: Sharjah Publishing City
Free Zone Sharjah, UAE.
Phone: 00971-551830334
Email : decanimprint@gmail.com

Cover Design & Layout : Siraj T.K.
Printed at :
Manipal Technologies Limited, Manipal.

ISBN 978-93-5973-397-5

Al Ameer English School, Ajman is a premier educational institution, founded and established in 1991 by a set of visionaries. The school is recognized by the Ministry of Education, UAE and affiliated to the Central Board of Secondary Education, New Delhi. Al Ameer aims at high standard of academic skills, inquisitive minds, psychosocial competencies and interpersonal skills of the students. The school offers a holistic learning programme for students of KG I to Grade XII.

It was all in a villa with 250 students, the school had its inception in 1991. Prince English School had its new name Al Ameer English School in 1999. With our strong determination, dedicated and committed team of teachers and other staff members, the school rose up to one of the best schools in the northern emirates.

The school is managed by the honourable Chairman Mr. A.K. Abdul Salam, a great visionary and philanthropist and is led by an eminent educationist Dr. S.J. Jacob. The strength of the school is devoted, committed and dedicated faculty, admin and other ancillary staff members.

The school has an enviable chain of records of academic success and excellence in co-curricular and extra-curricular activities. The school continuously produces excellent results, both at the secondary and senior secondary level examinations conducted by the CBSE with many of our students earning distinctions and first class positions in the exam results.

The School prepares the students with the 21st Century Skills to face the challenges of the ever-growing modern world. Creativity, communication, confidence-building, International Benchmark Assessments and value-based education are some of the highlights of the school.

Deccan Imprint Publishing co. Give importance to the project of **My School My Book is an activity** that emphasizes the creative processes in children. Many students of U.A.E have expressed their literary abilities through this project. Each school produces a book containing the writings of the students of their schools. This book contains a collection of writings by students of Ajman Al-Ameer School. Each of these articles confirms how imaginative the children have been in their writings. The book **Sparks of Insight** is dedicated to you.

With love
Team Deccan Imprint

Nurturing academic excellence...

I personally believe that an education system that develops the imagination of the child is richer than the one that does not. The imagination is where new ideas are created and progress becomes possible. "Imagination is more important than knowledge" because knowledge is about what we already know, whereas imagination is what moves individuals and cultures forward. Imagination leads to innovation. Evidently, our students have brought out their innovation and creativity through this book of their articles.

Hearty congratulations to all the budding authors!!!

The school records its sincere gratitude to the Honourable Sheikh H.H. Sultan bin Muhammad Al-Qasimi for their great interest in encouraging the Book Lovers through the Sharjah Book Fair, a Mega Event of the Era.

I would like to extend my words of appreciation and thanks to 'Deccan Publishing Company' and its key person Mr. Ashok Kumar for their wonderful initiative 'My School; My Book'.

My sincere thanks to the entire English Department and the HoD Ms Ancy Dileep for their sincere efforts and encouragement given to the students for this great work.

I hope the creativity of our younger generation continues to be kindled and unfolded at a maximum level for the sustainable development with the theme 'Today for Tomorrow'.

Dr. S. J. Jacob
Principal
Al Ameer English School, Ajman

A Glimpse into
excellence...

Dear Readers

It is with immense pride and excitement that I extend my heartiest congratulations to the team of English teachers and the student writers for the successful completion of this magazine. As we delve into the world of education and inspiration, I am reminded of the incredible journey we embark upon at Al Ameer English School. This book marks that our pursuit of knowledge is not merely confined to textbooks, it extends to nurturing character, creativity and critical thinking among our students.

The articles in this book stand as a testament to the dedication and hard work of our students and the unwavering support of our teaching fraternity.

With best regards

Mr Nowshad Shamsudeen
Vice Principal
Al Ameer English School, Ajman

If the book is true,
it will find an audience that is meant to read it...

I appreciate the entire team behind this endeavor for taking one step ahead on publishing this collection of articles.

I strongly believe that children should be motivated to grab every opportunity that comes their way which would not only help in their holistic growth but also strengthen their belief in collaborative learning. Congratulations dear students on this great opportunity and some of your articles are really thought provoking.

I would like to congratulate Mrs Ancy Dileep, HoD English for her tireless efforts to make this book happen in the form. Thanks to theteachers of English Department for guiding and motivating the students topresent refined articles.

Happy Reading !!!!!!

Mrs Latha Anil Warrier
Academic coordinator
Al Ameer English School, Ajman

"A professional writer is an amateur
who didn't quit."
– Richard Bach

I am writing to express my earnest appreciation for your outstanding compilation of articles on various topics that address the issues in order for a sustainable future. Your dedication, creativity, and enthusiasm in addressing the crucial topics are truly commendable.
Each article in your compilation reflects a deep understanding of the challenges we face in building a sustainable future. Your unique perspectives and well-researched content have shed light on various aspects of sustainability, the role of Science in making the world a better place to live in and the vision of youth for constructing a Global Unit for a peaceful living. I am enthralled by your passion for creating a better world and your commitment to raising awareness about sustainability issues.
I whole heartedly congratulate you on your achievements and encourage you to continue exploring and enhancing your writing skills. Your voices have the power to inspire others and make a tangible difference in our world. May you continue to embark on similar endeavors spreading knowledge that benefits the mankind.
Wishing you all the best in your future endeavours!

Geetha Narayanan
Supervisor (cycle-3)
Al Ameer English School, Ajman

A Writer only begins a book and a Reader finishes it...

As the Head of the English Department, I am delighted toexpress my sincere appreciation to the remarkable team of teachers and studentsfor their exceptional efforts in bringing forth a captivating book showcasingthe creativity of our students through their remarkable article writing.

The language skills displayed by our students are trulycommendable, reflecting their dedication and passion for their creative writing.I would also like to extend my gratitude to our diligent teachers, who workedtirelessly to refine the content and ensure its quality.

Lastly, I would like to thank our administrator for providingus with the opportunity to compile and publish this remarkable book. Iacknowledge the efforts of Mr Murali Mangalath who is pivotal in bringing outthis book. It is through the collaborative initiatives like this that we cancelebrate and nurture the talents of our students, fostering a love forliterature and language.

Congratulations to all involved in this endeavour, and maythis be the first of many such accomplishments to come!

Ancy Dileep
Head of English Department
Al Ameer English School, Ajman

The Vision of Youth for Global Politics

Abi Hazel

XI-A

Youth is the future of the nation....My focus is on the youth the youth!" said the political candidate in hiselection manifesto. The most comical irony is the fact that the politicianhimself is 60+! This is the unfortunate reality off the current globalpolitical scenario.

Politics is perhaps the only field when work starts only after retirement age. If we examine political leaders around the globe, the probability of finding black hair is close to zero! Let us take the example of India; a country with a booming youth population. The average age of the prime minister's cabinet is 55. The very cabinet that is supposed to take all the important decisions; decisions that can make or break the country and still, it is composed of members who are not at their mental peak. Age is just a number but when it is the question of the future and welfare of a billion people, every single detail matters. It is not that there is no youth in politics, it is just that they do not have access to meaningful positions. In India, the few young people who are into politics are looked down upon as 'hooligans', whose only purpose is to disrupt the peace & harmony and act like puppets of their party leaders.

If women have to be included in politics for women empowerment, if Dalits have to be included in politics for dalit empowerment, then surely the youth has to be included in politics for the empowerment of the entire nation, for isn't it them who swear that youth is the future of the nation? We need educated, energetic and enthusiastic men &women whose only motive is service to the people and not power or embezzlement of the national treasury. For that to happen, we need to make politics an attractive option for the youngsters; change its image from that of a power and money hungry corrupt war to that of a real competition for leadership &service. Only then can democracy, which is thrown around so frequently; can fulfil its actual meaning. If we cannot have 65 year old judges, 65 year old policemen, 65 year old bureaucrats; then surely we shouldn't also have 65 year old leaders!

The Vision Of UAE
For Sustainable Future

Adnan Mohammed
IX-C

The UAE is one of the leading countries for setting sustainable goals and making them happen. The UAE aims to be fully sustainable by 2050. This Article explores some key elements and highlights points for achieving sustainable goals.

Renewable Energy Revolution:
The use of petrol in the UAE is high. The UAE aims to recycle all of this energy and make it usable again. The UAE has planned to use 50% of its nuclear energy by 2050. The UAE is more focused on sustaining renewable energy.

Biodiversity preservation and conservation:
The UAE is looking forward to preserving animals that are weak and friendly. The UAE has built many sanctuaries for animals, such as the Arabian Oryx Sanctuary and the Mangrove Sanctuary. This shows the commitment of the UAE to preserving biodiversity. The UAE is one of the world's leading countries for biodiversity preservation and conservation. The UAE is preserving biodiversity for a sustainable

future and for the animals' needs.

Transportation and Mobility for Vehicles:
The use of gasoline-powered cars is high nowadays. The UAE is making more electric cars for a sustainable future. The UAE is making electric cars and reducing petrol-powered cars to prevent noise pollution and air pollution. All cars will be electric by 2050.

In conclusion, the UAE is a leading country for these key elements and points. The UAE is a pioneer in ensuring the sustainability of other countries.

Sustainable Future – UAE

Adwaith Arun Pillai
IX-A

The UAE is committed to achieving sustainable development to all its parts with its ambitious goal of becoming the most environmentally friendly country in the world. UAE has become the leading country in this field. The UAE's vision for a sustainable future is based on mainly 4 pillars: Economic Progress, Environmental -protection, educational development and responsible consumption and production.

To achieve its precise and lifesaving goal, the UAE has taken adequate initiatives that support a sustainable future. The country has encouraged young designers for more environmental architecture, same time this country has supporting and encouraging big industries to reduce its carbon footprint and to use more environmentally friendly alternatives like Solar and Wind Energy.

The UAE has also increased its water Industries to reduce the country's dependence on imported water. From the past many years UAE has practiced cloud seeding to increase its water resources and reduce the waste of water, these are the ideas that are still being used and practiced which require much less effort than the promising elephantine outcome it has on the environment. But UAE is still trying to figure out what to do with all that sand!

The UAE is home to many endangered animals like Arabian Oryx, Desert Rabbit, Yellow Fox and many more. Pollution has become very common and UAE is trying its level best to achieve a Sustainable future for all. Let the future be magnificent and wonderful, with clear skies, clean water and clean energy, available for all.

●

The UAE'S Vision
for Sustainable Future

Akhila Joseph Sequeira
X-B

Each day there sources are depleting. But UAE has its own solution for solving methods. UAEis a well-known developing country. For the past decades, this country has implemented goals for sustainable future. Sustainability means meeting the present needs without curtailing the future needs. Resources are referred to play vital role in human life that are economically feasible, culturally acceptable and technologically accessible. UAE has strongly versioned its country. A country with no poverty, with proper education and equality towards gender. According to the study, UAE is a developed country providing great infrastructure and a spectacular environment to everyone.

UAE has implemented 17 SDG (Sustainable Development Goals) for providing a secure future by the end of 2031. People from all over the world has collaborated with UAE just to ensure that no people will suffer for meeting their needs. For example, Madinah City in Abu Dhabi is a great example for sustainability. This city is referred to work with no electricity but with solar energy. UAE mainly focuses on renewable energy. As solar energy is a renewable energy ensuring that energy can be obtained using resources from our hands. UAE has taken initiative to promote sustainability through schools, so that students andtheir parents can take part in.

Hence, it's important to save our earth. UAE, a well developing country knows how it works. It's vision ensures a sustainable future for all to make sure that all have their equal rights, clean drinking water and food resources providing equal opportunities for both foreigners and Emiratis. Providing great infrastructure for all, ensuring that the country is moving along its right path. To provide a great future for the upcoming years for the people, as sustainable development plays a vital role in human being to conclude that the resources, we use now are not borrowed from our forefathers but are borrowing from our future.

●

The Vision of Youth in Global Politics

Amrita Shajikumar

XII-B

There was always a time when politics were constrained to only experienced and elderly people but now there is a great change in it. Nowadays youth shows their interest to voice out in politics.

Youth in politics will provide more betterment for the public as today's youth are well aware of the happenings and have an aim for working towards their country's success. Youth very well know the issues faced by public as they also the part of public and face it. The youth may not have great experience as other elderly leaders but still they might have the courage to take up and work for it. There are lots of countries promoting youth in politics, some of those countries are Nigeria, Azerbaijan, Bangladesh and so on. These countries create youth political committee and they discuss and work for the public. Nowadays youth face certain issues like depression and mental health illness, so if youth comes in charge they can give awareness and take certain measures on these.

To sum up, the youth must be encouraged to participate in world politics as it will provide an uplift to all the countries. The youth can also do a lot for the public and in future we can all witness the best world politics.

Role of Science in
Making New India

Aniqa Shoeb
VI-B

Science has a major role in shaping the world as it is today. Science enables us to know more and more about the things that exist around us. It is because of science that we have been able to use resources present in nature. If we compare present with the five years back period, we will certainly see many changes indiscoveries and technological inventions.

Science hasled to numerous inventions and technological advancement in different sectors of the nation. The agriculture is gifted with many enormous tools and machines which have reduced the labors and made the work easier and very faster. All the sectors of India are benefitted from the emergence of science. The advancement in tools and machines made the agricultural process easy. Medical fields are also doing great jobs with the emergence of science and technology. New Application inventions have made our daily life easy and comfortable. Science is also helping in the development of space and research fields. People are connected with the advent of science. Science is contributing in uplifting India in many ways.

The Vision of Youth for Global Politics

Arjun Kishore

XII-A

In today's rapidly changing world, the voices of young people are resonating louder than ever before, driving a transformative vision for global politics. As the leaders of the future, the youth have embraced a progressive mindset, demanding more inclusive, sustainable and equitable systems.

One crucial aspect of the youth's vision for global politics is a call for greater representation. They advocate for increased participation of youth in decision-making processes at all levels, recognising the importance of different perspectives in making policies that affect their lives. By promoting inclusivity, the young people aim to bridge the gap between generations. Another key focus of youth's vision is sustainability. Concerned about the environmental challenges faced by the planet, young activists are at the forefront of demanding immediate action to mitigate climate change, preserve bio diversity, and ensure a sustainable future for generations to come. They support green initiatives, renewable energy and responsible consumption, aiming to reshape the global politics with a strong focus on environmental conservation.

Furthermore, the youth's vision for global politics highlights social justice and equality. They strive to eradicate systemic discrimination, inequality and poverty. They support human rights, gender equality and inclusivity. Their goal is to create a world where every individual, regardless of their background, has equal opportunities to thrive and contribute to society.

In conclusion, the vision of youth for global politics is marked by a determination to create a more inclusive, sustainable and just world. They demand greater representation, prioritize environmental conservation and advocate for social equality. As their influence grows, the young people are reshaping the politics, offering afresh perspective and inspiring hope for a brighter future. Their vision for global politics serves as a powerful reminder that the collective voice of youth is a force to be considered with in shaping a better world.

●

The Vision of Youth for Global Politics

Asniya Nowshad
XII-B

Global Politics is not just some letters; it is the words of a youth's vision. A political perspective to sustain the world 'a youth today is the leader for tomorrow', and it's their vision that turns into reality. Global economic hardship, an increase in temperature, the Ukraine crisis, and the African drought are just a few to realize. Having a cognizance of global politics is easy, but to voice it is the real question. Global politics is the political globalization of social power. Here, the vision to edify is human rights, Sovereignty, Development, Pacifism, peace, conflicts, and liberalization on the global front—those to be debated.

The world is bewildered as to how to face challenges like Climate change, in which the moderate climate our ancestors experienced has rapidly changed with a significant increase in temperature, becoming warmer, wetter, and drier. Even can't be forecasted - all because of the US. Emissions of CO_2 in excess, overuse of minerals, melting of ice, and acid rain are a few. It's important to point out that she has broken the record in the year 2020 by an average of 55 degrees Celsius and that this is just the beginning. "You are never too small to make a difference"—a vision of 20-year-old environmental activist Greta Thunberg says it all. If she can, why can't we? Wars play a pivotal role in bringing down the peace of the world, like in Ukraine-Russia. 'Ukraine and Russia trade places to battle in Bukhurt' and 'Russian Invasion with Tanks' are all over the headlines. Thousands were lost, injured, and destroyed, yet stuck on their guns. There is much to question about the existence of humanity, peace, and liberalization. These are just two of many, to combat these perilous situations. Global warming is the key.

As the development grows, so does the need to sustain it. I am proud to mention that there has been some initiative by countries, like celebrating this year as the Year of Sustainability in the United Arab Emirates, the United States of America passing the inflation Bill, and the UNICEF Law on Africa, all to create a sense of responsibility for the Youth. Expand the vision, they say, but it is to point out that too much power to youth without the right adult assistance could turn over, but it's never too late to raise your voice, have alternatives, question it, and fulfill your vision.

There have also been diploma programs for youth in Global politics in which they could participate, as well as the 2030 Agenda, which gives the youth complete participation in the SDGs. If it's the future to be redeemed, it's from the youth's perspective, not just some high words above, but the words of a high vision for an inequality-free, strife-free, harmonious, and tranquil world to come—all worth a step by the youth for a better future.

●

The Golden Sparrow's
Biggest Secret of Being a Developed
Country revealed!!

Aysha Farzeen

VII - D

Some kind of force is helping India. India has been getting and giving birth to new technologies and innovations. This new found technology has been helping India. Be it medicines field, strengthening the defence system and much more. All of these achievements are being accomplished with the help of "science".

Science has been helping India for so long. Have you even known that science is the reason that India is on its verge of becoming a developed country. No goods can be transferred from one place to another without the aid ofscience. This science is also helping doctors and medical researchers to find the cure for diseases that could ever let as soul rest in peace. Oldest medicine system, chakra Samhita was a team stire ayurveda, Indian's Oldest medical branch. But know without all these ancient methods we can find virtually and determine what is happening inside us. It is all because of science. Science makes it all possible for us to communicate with each other across the world. This not only grows the relationship between people but also gives birth to opportunities on an international level.

India would be still in its early stages. So, if you still think that you will stop science from elementary education then rethink, because a developed country like India used one and only powerful weapon in this world. So, if you want to contribute to your country, then choose science. A subject and a reason why India is on its peek today.

●

The Vision of Youth for Global Politics

S. Mohammed Ayyoub

XII-A

We live in a generation that calls for a new and improved system of politics. There are numerous young men and women that collectively, and individually aspire to rejuvenate and remodel our system of unfair and imbalanced politics.

There have been initiatives taken by the world as a whole even today, to improve our planet's condition by spreading global warming and climate change awareness. These phenomena are recognized today as an immediate threat to our existence.

Climate change awareness and international cooperation is one of these goals that every visionary young man and woman desires. Deforestation, The Complete abolishment of the use of fossil fuels, and the development of renewables are important initiatives that require immediate development. As a former foreign minister of Sweden, Margot Wall strom said, "There is no sustainable development, without Sustainable energy development."

But the quality that really, any person needs is Honesty. Politics as of today is accustomed to bribery, dishonesty, corruption, and injustice. But the future is somewhere that ideas of corruption may not succeed. Humanity can only develop further if it is rid of its greed.

The planet requires good, sustainable leaders, and those leaders will be from our generation. So we must all improve ourselves and believe in each other. So that someday one of us will lead humanity in the right direction.

•

The Vision of Youth for Global Politics

Benet Anna Anil
XII-B

Youth and politics - a topic often seen with exorbitant controversy. Youth is the future. They are today's seedlings that will one day become tomorrow's tree. In them we see what we have in hold for the future. They show us a lot of ideals that could potentially change the world. They have a growing mind that is filled with curiosity, ideas and so much more that we didn't even discover some of it yet.

Youth has a very vital role in politics and in the evolving world. They helped the world in many circumstances. For instance, during the Second World War, most soldiers who fought upfront formed the youth. In another occurrence, Greta Thunberg, along with several other members of the youth, sued the Swedish government for the climate crisis in their country. In Kerala, India, during the worst flood of the century, it was the youth who showed up in times of others' need. The growing generation has visions that are not often brought out due to lack of opportunities. People under the age of 35 are found very rarely in politics. As a result, governments across the world are opening up more and more chances for them. They could have a revolutionary mindset that is not given the chance to speak up and these mindsets could potentially lead to a better future, a better country and a better home. Their minds have to be opened to the world outside of their homes, to show them the endless possibilities that the future has in store for them. They also have to be shown their capabilities and how much they could have put use to it.

We are in desperate need of people who are willing to solve our problems and the youth is the first step to it. But for that, we need to promote and encourage them. We should also teach and show them the right ways. Yes, politics is a field that is hard to work and progress in, but it is not a field that does not land them in ways that can change them and the world that we live in. Just like how butterflies, even though beautiful creatures, do not have a clear vision of their wings, we still have not figured out what the youth has hidden in their treasure chests.

●

The Vision of Youth for Global Politics

Bestin Roy

XII-A

Indeed, the world is led by renowned leaders aging over 60s. In fact, the average age of world leaders as of right now is 59.2. This result in world leaders who may be out of touch and make decisions that the youth don't approve. This has been the case since way back, as people tend to believe that older people are more capable in politics due to their experience. While this is true to an extent, youth must also be involved in global politics. Young people tend to have lot of ideas and wider vision compared to the old people. Youth are also more open-minded. But due to the attitude of the seniors in politics and the people towards youth when it comes to politics, they don't get a chance. They then end up exactly like old people, limited in vision and narrow minded. Things are changing for the good however. The average age of world leader has been reducing and there is more involvement of youth in global politics. There is still more work to be done though. The youth should be given more chance as they have so much to offer to the world. The perfect mix for the improvement of global politics is the experience of old people and the ideals and vision of the youth.

Scientific Advancement in New Age India

Devapriya Rajesh

VIII-D

Life is really a game of days. In this world of inimitable competition and strenuous achievements, a nation needs to be well advanced in order to prosper well in the global arena. India is now very much moving in that direction and the role of scientific temper and passionate young aspirants proved to be vital symbols of our future.

During the last few years, India has proven its scientific prowess in different arenas such as space, defence system, agriculture, health care etc... India is the first country to reach the Mars orbit in the first attempt using the "Mangalyan". It was India's first interplanetary mission. If we move onto the field of defence system, India is not far behind. India has indigenous designs and has immerse development capacity on state-of-the-art warfare and defence mechanism. India has also proven its skills in the realms of agriculture. In the primitive times, the farmers used methods that were time consuming and exhausting but now with the indigenization of science and technology their work has become easier because of new modern facilities like texting cows, irrigational system etc....Lastly, when the phenomenon of Covid 19 had swept the world off its feet, India stood up and made not only one, but two vaccines and inoculated 75 percent of its population. It is truly an unimaginable thing.

In conclusion, with the in digenisation of science and technology, India has changed from being an impoverished nation into being a well-equipped and developed country. I am not being presumptuous about anything I say but I truly believe that science has turned India into a whole new country.

Science is the essential key for the prosperity of India!

Emaan Iqbal

VIII-B

Science has a very big impact on India, both in terms of social and economic basis. As Science grows so does India.

Science has helped India build satellites and send probes to moon and mars. As Science develops India becomes newer and has all types of changes through Science. Science is known as the essential key for making new India. Science helps India make more inventions, which makes India famous, powerful and unique. "Ayurveda" is known as "Science of life", It has been practised and still is for over 5000 years in India. The new inventions that Science brings to India helps India in making it new , brilliant and so much more . Science in India has grown a lot in India in the past few years and the way Science impacts India has grown a lot more than how it did before. Science is the reason India is in the state it is in now. Science has helped India create vaccines, medicines and newer technology.

Science has made the new India and has proved in terms of medicine, vaccines, machine's, which has made India unique and famous. The way Science has made India better is the reason for the great state of India and its happy citizens.

Role of science in making new India

Evelyna Joshy
VIII-B

Science is necessary in all spheres of life. Just like we saywithout mathematics world is a complete zero, Science is no exception. Every country should invest in development of Science and technology. Today, this article is going to explain how science is important in the progress of India.

Science has helped India in providing job opportunities to unemployed people in our country. When some invention is made, it requires professionals to perfect it. Thus, people are employed and India will make an immense growth economically. When people get new job opportunities, India will also grow fast in scientific fields. Another role of science is in making medicine and curing people from diseases. Science plays a major role in making medicines. With the advancements of science in medical field, people get cured even from deadly diseases. It also helps in surgeries, transplants and other medical operations.

Another place where science is important is agricultural sector. Science has already proved to be essential because farmers used traditional methods of agricultural practices which was time-

consuming, expensive, and hard labour. With the help of Science, modern agricultural methods are used and it increases the growth of crops, saves time and labour.

For a country to progress, science plays a very important role. From making medicines, inventing something, to developing a country, science is not just necessary but is also compulsory. So, I hope you understand how science is important in developing India and making it a reliable and a modern place. In the progressing of a country, Science is undeniable.

●

The Vision Of UAE
For Sustainable Future

Fadi Aman

IX-A

The United Arab Emirates (U.A.E) is a Leading Inspiration for Sustainable development or for the vision of a sustainable future for the country. U.A.E has become a Global Model for making the Year "2023" as the Year of Sustainability. It has also created a famous tagline for the year that is "today for tomorrow". Actually, the Sustainable development means the development that takes place without harming the environment or Natural Resources for the future generation. This is itself the reason why U.A.E has made the icon "Today for tomorrow"means that how we use the resources today will affect tomorrow or the future generations. U.A.E is a leading country in its advancement of technology and the modern infrastructure. If U.A.E hasn't made a vision like this the country's economic state would get completely changed.

The Five Visions that U.A.E took at the aim of Sustainable Future are as follows:
1. Renewable Energy Resource Revolution: U.A.E has large areas of Deserts and the temperature of U.A.E is very high. So as for the

Sustainable Future Visions U.A.E has decided to make the Electricity Powered by Solar Panels. One Among the World's largest Solar Plantation is in U.A.E that is Mohammed Bin Rashid Al-Maktoum Solar plantations in U.A.E. By this plantation the leaders of U.A.E aim to generate75% of Dubai's energy from renewable sources by 2050. Additionally, the U.A.E has been at the forefront of promoting nuclear energy, with the Barakah Nuclear Energy Plant becoming the first nuclear power plant in the Arab world. According to the visions of U.A.E for a sustainable future Dubai in 2050 willbe an Emirate with electricity from solar plants.

2. Urban Planning for Sustainability: U.A.E has made a unique city in Abu Dhabi known as Masdar City. In this unique city there are places for practice of Sustainable development, there are green buildings, technological infrastructure etc.

3. Bio diversity Conservation: Even though U.A.E is a hot desert there are animals which are endangeredand coral reserves to protect. The Arabian oryx sanctuary and the AL WATHBA WET LAND RESERVE, MANGROVE CONSERVATION, CORAL REFORMS are some of the reserved areas for biodiversity protection or conservation in U.A.E.

4. Water Scarcity. Due to the hot sun and lack of Rainfall the amount of water is very less. So, U.A.E has started destination Water Plantation in Jabel Ali and has taken strict measures to conserve Water

5. Agricultural Practices: As due to the sandy soil in U.A.E. Agriculture is tough but still agricultureis practised through various methods like vertical farming and hydroponics they have made farming possible. These the Various Reforms or Visions of the U.A.E for a Sustainable future. U.A.E is paving way for a greener future. It has Invested a lot in the use of Electric Vehicles and advancement of technology etc. The leaders of U.A.E have taken Certain decision to make the country a Sustainable country.

●

The Vision of UAE
for Sustainability

Fathima Lasheen

IX-B

The UAE plays an important role in the Global Sustainability. Sustainability means providing one's needs and making it a better country for the future generation. The sustainability was introduced by His Highness Sheikh Mohammed Bin Rashid Al Maktoum, Vice President of the UAE. The UAE is focusing on goal 7, goal 8 and goal 17 for sustainability development. The UAE focuses on ending all types of poverty by 2030.

The UAE is ranked 11th on having sustainability environment. The UAE plans on making ranked 1st on sustainability development. There are 12 STD's which focuses on making UAE a better country. 44% clean energy, 38% gas and 12% clean coal. The country focuses on making everything based on technology and solar powers. The UAE wants to make everything based on solar panel for sunlight and is trying to make better quality on air and stop pollution. The 1st ever build city based on sustainability is Masdar City, Abu Dhabi-UAE, that will finish its progress by2030. In the Masdar City, no cars are allowed, and there is pathway for walking and metro train. For sunlight, they depend upon solar panels. The theme of the UAEfor 2023 is "Today for

Tomorrow". The plastic will be stopped soon in UAE as it pollutes the country.
The UAE wants everyone to come together and spread the word "Sustainability". The UAEis an inspiration for the term "Work Hard and You Will Achieve it".

●

The Vision of Youth for Global Politics

Girikrishna Gireeshkumar
XII-C

Youth plays a major role in today's world of politics. They work together to create an upcoming generation of people who will respect each other despite their education, race, and no other discrimination. The youth also values the climatic conditions just as the problems and conflicts among human beings.

Youth is the catalysts for change. They are focused on changing the environment for the best. They provide opportunities for the younger generation to speak up, to know their opinions etc. Youth is at the forefront of climate change. They demand meaningful action from decision-makersand policymakers for sustainable practices and for investing in renewable energy. Their vision encompasses a global political system that prioritizes sustainability.

The youth are against discrimination, and they strive to create a community that is committed to combating social justice and inequality. They envision a world that eliminates discrimination based on race and gender.

The challenges faced by young people in the field of global politics are that they have limited representation. Youth often face barriers to political participation, including age restrictions, lack of representation and limited access to the decision-making process. Their vision calls for an inductive political system that actively involves protecting their environment.

Thus, it is important for the young people to step into the field of politics because everyone living on the earth wants a world which celebrates diversity, promotes peace and equality and those who ensure a sustainable development for both the present and future young generation.

●

From Lab to Land :
How Science revolutionized India .

Gowri Rajeev
VII-D

India, a land of diversity and cultural richness has always been at the forefront of scientific innovation. Science inIndia has made various vital contribution. Its impact has greatly effected our country. From ancient times to modern day advancements, science in India has come a long way.

India has made remarkable contributions ove rthe past few decades. One of the most notable development is India's space program which has launched more than 100 satellites into orbit. In 2019, India became the fourth country to successfully test an anti satellite weapon showcasing it's technological capabilities on a global level. In recent years, India has also became a leader in renewable energy technologies. With ambitious targets set , greater renewable energy sources like solar powers which has been efficient and cost effective developed. The malfunctioning of Vaccines from Indian Emprises provides low-cost and efficient vaccines which has made the life of common people easier and made India, a key factor on the globe .

Science continues to provide a significant effect on us . By continuing this trajectory through sustained investments ; we can expect greater achievements making India, Our Country, a global leader for Science and Technology Advancement.

The Vision of Youth for Global Politics

Hanna Anwar
XII-B

In the recent decades , participation of youth in politics has been decreased alarmingly. The youth should be encouraged to participate in the politics for the betterment of the society.

Important strikers such as Martin Luther King, Barack Obama, Mahatma Gandhi had put their efforts forward to make the world we are living in peaceful. If these people had not made an effort in helping our world, the condition would have been unimaginable. We are able to enjoy the freedom, justice, equality etc just because they have shown courage to step up for the loss of their own lives, for the future generations to be free from the hell of a world. Rosa Park, a famous striker, if she had not step up for the seat in her bus. We would have not been able to sit or travel in public transports without being discriminated based on our skin colour. The young generation is asked to participate in promoting global politics for a better tomorrow. When we allow them to voice their opinions in the talk of the world, we are exposed to various new ideas that helps in shaping our future, allowing them to enjoy their life without being oppressed under unreasonable laws.

The youth is pushed to put forward their opinions and ideas for a sustainable environment. They should be aware of the condition of the world around them and not just being active on social media. Posters, articles, awareness should be provided for them to understand the importance of their involvement in politics, like how you are reading this article which may be confusing but is an important topic in today's world to maintain a sustainable future. Efforts taken today will be presented tomorrow.

The Vision of Youth for Global Politics

Laya Sai
XII-B

Participation of youth, their innovative ideas and extensive thoughts are some factors which immensely contribute to the development of the country. The future of youth decides the future of a nation.

Their thoughts and voices are important to build a nation. As the population, so does the youth. Many of the countries utilizes this factor to enhance the development of the country. The active participation of the youth increases the enhancement of several factors which a country requires to be termed as developed. Youth played important roles in global politics. About 60% of youth fought world war in favour to Germany. Youth were there during natural calamities and other disastrous events to lend helping. they were the ones to initiate a program or awareness which contribute to the development of the country. Countries like Japan develops rapidly as they give chance for youth to present their ideas and thoughts for the betterment of the country.

Youth is considered significant for the betterment of a country. The government should give chance to each person to express their ideas and thoughts so that a great change can be brought to country and its people.

Sustainability and UAE's Vision towards it.

Leona Bijoy
IX-B

We all have heard of the word "Sustainability" before but what exactly is sustainability? Sustainability is the ability to develop without exhausting natural resources. Therefore, sustainable future isthe development that meets the needs of the present without compromising the needs of the future generation.

This sustainable development goals(SDGS) were introduced in 2015 to help protect natural resources and to achieve a sustainable future. It is a "Shared blue printfor peace and prosperity for the people and the planet now and into the future."There are 17 sustainable development goals (SGDS) including gender equality, quality education etc. The SDGS aim to end all forms of poverty and hunger in the world by 2030. Now what is UAE's vision towards a sustainable future? The UAE government highlighted its commitment towards achieving the sustainabledevelopment goals and improving the lives of the people as part of globaldevelopment efforts. The UAE focuses on achieving all the SDGS as all the issues still exist in the country. The country believes that the sustainable development goals aim at supporting communities and improving people's lives. The UAE has achieved significant achievements for sustainable development goals and has been recognised by major international organisations. The UAE has ranked number 1 in 97 indexes relating to SDGS. Here are two of UAE's sustainable development projects:

   i. Masdar City (Abu Dhabi)
■ Masdar City is one of the most prominent sustainable urban development projects in the Middle East.
■ Masdar City uses technology and solar power to reduce energy wastage and usage of water.
   ii. Sustainable City (Dubai)
■ It is an eco-friendly project that focuses on social, economic and environmental sustainability.
■ It has a nature-based architecture and is an example of how sustainable development is making the city more environment-friendly.

The UAE is moving in the right direction and ensuring development comes with environment and not at the cost of it by these projects. The UAE continues to pave its way for a sustainable future.

●

The Vision of Youth for
Global Politics

Maliha Arjumand
XI-B

A county's youth are the major agents of its development. The way they visualize their future eventually goes on to become the future of the world. Their dreams, thoughts, and aspirations contribute significantly to a country's progress. However, according to the United Nations (UN), in 2022, two out of every three countries will not consider young people in aspects like poverty reduction or decision-making.

The International Republican Institute (IRI) has recently launched a global program called 'Generation Democracy', which aims at providing a platform for the younger generations to mobilize their peers and discuss solutions to global issues.

This program is being carried out in more than 70 countries across the globe. The visions of youth might differ from country to country or region to region, but their goal is one—to be able to have a role in politics as much as the older people.

As per a survey conducted by the United Nations, most young people express a need for educational, social, and political modernization. Many consider the educational status of their leaders and technological advancement to play a major role in the development of global politics. Apart from this, secularism and the end of racism are the main topics that youth of today are seen rising constantly. Many young people in Afghanistan, Somalia, Nigeria, and Uganda are seen raising their voices against poverty and repression. They feel that unless other countries come together at the global level to help them, there can be no improvement in their conditions. The visions of youth at different places vary, but their goals and aspirations for a better democracy remain the same.

All of this has been noticed by world leaders. Since the past two decades, several efforts have been made to increase the role of youth in politics. The United Nations has declared 2022 "The Year of Youth". Now, young people are getting a platform to express their ideas as global citizens, even though their role in politics remains minimal. And as a wise man has rightly stated,

"The future of today depends on the youth of tomorrow."

●

The Vision of Youth for
Global Politics

Manjima Reena Manoj
XII-B

The youth's participation in global politics has always faced contradictions. Though they are a strong driving force, capable of bringing change, yet statistics show that they are least likely to vote in elections and show less or no interest in politics. Due to the recent geopolitical changes and issues, there has been a change to this.

Youth has always been a helping factor throughout ages. Their role in the Indian freedom struggle is very much appreciated. This generation has seen and endured the collapse of governments, evils of corruption, struggles of unemployment, poverty and world hunger. This has led them to live with certain principles and visions for the future. They have dynamic strategies and ambitions and goals and visions which if implemented could change the face of global politics. They are high- driven and ambitious and this was seen in Sweden when a network of children sued the State for declining their plan of action against climate change, and in mass protests against the CAA bills in Delhi. The youth today are confident enough to voice out their opinion.

The participation of youth in global politics can be achieved only by providing opportunities. The societal pressure to take up engineering and medical science as career options have silenced many youths. They should be given an opportunity to voice out their concerns. Their ideas of eradicating unemployment, provide education, end world hunger and corruption etc. should be given a chance to be implemented and spread. Those that believe and are confident about making a change should be given opportunities, and high positions in the government. Vision and strategies of youth are very important and necessary. Their visions on how to make a difference and end major world problems need to be heard and implemented. The youth are indeed the leaders of tomorrow. They are the key to a better, peaceful world and their visions and goals pave a way to make global politics reach its extreme glory. Political leaders should harness the youth to solve problems, rather than create it. The vision of youth for global politics could actually make a difference. Thank You.

●

The Vision of Youth for Global Politics

Maryam Saidu
XII-D

Politics is one of the most prominent backbones of any economy. As far as Global politics is concerned, it isn't confined to politics of only the government. It is multi-dimensional and constantly invites new views and decisions for growth on a macro scale. The prevailing misconception is that the youth of the world doesn't own fruitful visions for economy and politics. However, history proves it wrong. Drawing an example towards a vast country like India, the youngest Prime Minister, Rajiv Gandhi, was forty years old when he took the oath. He proceeded to make changes in India through technology.

In the modern world, gender politics has been a revolutionary debate since 2020. Today's youth aspires to make changes in politics and economics while keeping a socialistic view. Global politics of Gen Z and millennials are highly driven by empathy and mutual respect. Thus, modern global politics doesn't keep up a vision of violent wars or secret games.

Another area in which Gen Z has been acting on is the 8-hour workday.

In the 1920's, workers protested to reduce nine hours of work a day into eight hours, making productive changes in politics. The youth is often misunderstood and underestimated as incapable political leaders, when IQ, EQ and many other factors are measured in concern with age. In reality, the youth analyzes the real needs of the economy and strives to make changes through politics. Their learning mentality leads them to think from an open and wide point of view. Thus, their vision for global politics is for better standards of living, and promoting an overall sense of mental maturity among their people. This vision could be carried out by many means- that includes social media, poetry or even prisons.

The power of decision making isn't granted to many; but as history proves, the youth of the generation has always struggled their way to voice out their opinions in global politics. The vision and spirit they cherish in their hearts still isn't appreciated by many. However, global politics has always only flourished under leaders with vision and undying passion.

The Vision of Youth for Global Politics

Mariyam Fayiza Aliyu
XII-B

The vision of youth for the global politics is driven by the statistics of the younger generation whose aspirations even can bring changes in the world. They want to see more women, more people of colors, LGBTG+ communities on the front line of the politics.

Further more, they want people who bring the change in the sustainability development, economic development and bring out the new minds and change for the better and quality living for the world as the controversies include so many build up for the lifestyle. Bringing the change cannot be done by one but the leaders should march up on the issues faced by the people bring out the hidden opinions and others voices out so to create a different landscape.

In conclusion, as far the world we see we don't need a nationalism but the global cooperation. Where to sustain and express the views and excellence for wide range and build differently the young minds with bring out the positive vibes and ring the bell of every people out there. They have the rights to motivate and have the rights to bring out the different degree of mindset in this living space.

The Vision of Youth for Global Politics

Meghana Ratheesh
XII-B

Youth - creative, enthusiastic, and passionate part of modern society can play an important role in resolving global issues. The vision of the educated youth is generally straightforward and direct to the society in which they are part of.

Global political issues mainly include environmental stewardship, international war, global trade, and human rights. In the case of environmental stewardship, many countries are now encouraging sustainability for preserving nature for the future generation. Youth can come forward by sharing their ideas and opinions to protect their surroundings and to preserve. When it comes to international wars, there are yet many unresolved conflicts between many international countries. The government should accept the thoughts of youth in these matters since they have a much higher sense about the inequalities going around. In the case of Global trade, the rise in prices of commodities or a major decrease, can affect society as a whole and our youth have a greater knowledge about these, and they must come up with new initiatives for equality in global markets. When it comes to human rights, many parts of the world are suffering from issues like improper education, poverty, lack of freedom and many other issues. Youth must be able to put their thoughts into action and encourage others for the community.

Youth is indeed an asset of every country, and the government must surely consider their thoughts and actions. The vision of youth is mostly regarding the society in which they strive, and they must take a step forward. As the great Martin Luther King said, "I have a dream and I believe that one day it will be realized, and young people will play one of the main roles in this process".

●

The vision of UAE
for sustainability

Meha Zainab
IX-B

The sustainable development goals (SDG) or the global goals is a set of 17 goals that aim to provide better living conditions to the people. The SDGs are based of the United Nations Millennium Development Goals.The SDGs are part of the 2023's agenda for sustainability. The UAE is taking several methods to achieve SDGs in homes and abroad.

The emirate of Abu Dhabi has taken several visions to ensure sustainability. One of them being the environment vision 2030. This vision for Abu Dhabi was developed to ensure integration of the three pillars of sustainability; environment, economic and social visions. The main aim ofthis vision is to preserve the cultural heritage of the emirate along with using its resources for better living conditions of the people. Another vision is the Abu Dhabi Economic vision 2030. The government of Abu Dhabi announced along term plan for the transformation of the emirate's economy. This plan included limitations on reliance on oil sectors and a greater focus on knowledge-based industries for the future.

The emirate of Dubai has also put up several strategies for SDG. The Dubai Industrial Strategy being one of them. in 2016 June, the vice president of UAE and the ruler of Dubai Sheikh Mohammed launched the Dubai Industrial Strategy to elevate Dubai into a global platform for knowledge based, sustainable, innovation focused business. The Dubai industrial Strategy has five main objectives, that will serve as the foundation of Dubai's industrial future. The strategy further identifies six-priority sub-sectors that were chosen based on their importance to Dubai Industrial strategy and Dubai plan 202. Another strategy is the Dubai Autonomous and Transportation Strategy. The main aim ofthis strategy is to transform 25 percent of Dubai's total transportation into Autonomous mode by 2030.

The UAE is taking several steps and doing its best to ensure SDGs in houses and abroad. We can learn from this country to use the resources, but not to an extent where there is none left for the future generations.

●

The Vision of UAE
for a Sustainable Future.

Minnah Akbar
IX-D

"We are building a new reality for our people, a new future for our children, and anew model of development."
-HisHighness Sheikh Mohammad Bin Rashid, Vice President and the Ruler of Dubai.

Thesewords were said by the ruler of Dubai. Aren't the goals set to be achieved?Well, so is the sustainable development goals. What is sustainable development? What is a Sustainable Future for the UAE? Sustainable Development is a type of development in which the needs of the present are fulfilled without compromising the ability of the future generation to meet their needs. A country must develop, but on the path of development, never forget about thefuture. While bringing economic changes, it's advised to use renewable sources of energy and limitedly approach for non - renewable sources of energy.

What visions have the UAE set towards sustainability? Numerous in one word. UAE has been trying to ban the use of plastic, growing mangroves in Abu Dhabi and somuch more. The UAE keeps on developing new infrastructure, new road networks and many more. Due to this rapid development UAE could run out of resources. To prevent this kind of a run out, the UAE have set up many goals and visions for the beautiful future. In the distant future, many counties may run out of fresh water. Studies and researches show that, by 2030 freshwater could run out if we use it at the current rate of careless consumption. Sustainable Development Goal number 14; "Conserve and sustainably use oceans, seas and marine resource for sustainable development" may not be achieved if we pollute the water resources in the current manner. Use of petroleum has been skyrocketing. If we run out of petroleum or other types of fuels, there will be no more cars which power using fuels. That is why, Electric cars are being introduced. UAE is taking huge initiatives insustainable development which must be appreciated.

What does humans do to promote a sustainable living? Nothing! Humans waste and pollute water and use fossil fuels carelessly. The stakes of our future generation struggling is really high. We have to think above and beyond to protect the future. Enjoying the fact that we have so much resources that have made human beings lazy to do anything towards sustainable development. Let's look forward to a future where people don't have to struggle.

The Vision of Youth for Global Politics

Musaffa Khanam
XII-B

In this time and age, youngsters have been able to achieve anything they've set their minds upon. They hold the power to dream, to have a vision, and change the world for the better. Now imagine if this extraordinary vision was set to make a global change. Today's youth has shown confidence, courage and desire to make their views and opinions heard, weather it be through social media, campaigns or even through their love of writing and speaking.

This magnificent yet complicated world is run by rules, regulations and the people of everyone's own country. History has made us aware of the ugly conflicts from the beginning of life. Looking around now, from the comfort of our home, we are in peace. We live in harmony. Safe to say this is what global politics is all about. The relations between countries and different borders to be in peace and find common ground is global politics. However, when I say 'the comfort of our homes' I unfortunately leave out the numerous groups that live a life not worthy to be even called a 'life'. Global politics is not all sunshine and roses. Like the past, conflicts have risen even in the present. And it's the people; innocent people who suffer. THIS is where the vision of our youth comes in handy. The new generation has grown to be more tolerant, more accepting of culture, ideas, opinions, but most importantly of people's rights. They firmly believe that they can make a better future, devoid of wars and hatred. They believe no man must suffer and fear his life. And they are not afraid to speak. Over the past few years, we have seen many young people expressing their views against conflicts and stand against the government itself. Take Greta Thunberg for example. She has shown remarkable resilience and inspired millions of people to do what is right for this world. This youth can do anything they wish for. They can and will help countless countries achieve peace and solitude. All because they care about their children's futures, and what we can achieve together.

There is a fine line between good and bad, right or wrong, love and hate. This youth will show the world that through their consistent efforts and strong voices, their vision, their hopes will come through. And there is no force of nature strong enough to beat them.

●

The Vision of Youth for
Global Politics

Noora Sulthana Nizam
XI-D

With vision, the mind manifests its mission. By joining the elements of vision, mindset, manifestation and mission, an individual can easily move from conceptualizing a future to taking a practical step to make it a reality.

It is completely necessary to understand that the vision of youth for global politics is diverse as individuals prioritize issues and give preferences to certain changes based on their experiences. But the key thread that runs through their minds related to global politics can be inclusivity and equality, which defines as the transparency of politics and equality for representation regardless of non-materialisticcharacters.

Youth have another aim for global politics: peaceful conflict resolution through dialogues, ethics and non-violence. Security and human rights are the most important concept youth strive for. The youth also emphasize the need for the world to sustainable living and global politics to take care of resource management, energy saving, and sustainability to provide a better future for the generations to come.

Youth craves global politics with greater participation and

opportunities i.e., global politics that values and accepts youth's necessities and demands. Youths can be considered the assets of global politics as they highlight the ability of technology to shape better politics. It's always better to provide seats to the children of any nation as they are the future of the same.

●

The Vision of Youth for
Global Politics

Ram Prasanna M.K.
XII-A

Youth as we know are the future generations on which the world depends on. The problems that are faced by the youth like unemployment, illiterate, global issues etc... has brought the world to concern. Involvement of youth is necessary to boost up economy and enrich the wealth of the nation. Youth's involvement is required in many global issues.

Our world has changed a lot in the past few years ,the invention of new technologies has created new opportunities and made our tasks easier, but unfortunately there are many issues and problems that challenges us. The challenges that the modern world faces are :

1. Climatechange
2. Globalconflict (lack of unity).
3. Global poverty
4. Biodiversityloss
5. Scarcity ofResources etc.

Youth'sinvolvement is very much necessary in climate change action as we know that there is an increase in our planet's temperature and many countries reported the impacts that the residents feel due to climate change. countries like Kiribati, Australia, etc. Kiribati a pacific island with an 100,000 in habitantsis expected to be missing from the world map by 2100. We need the support of youth as they have more innovative ideas to develop our planet. Peace keeping is another very important aspect to lead a peaceful life. Unlike the conflicts which recently took place like Russia and Ukraine conflict affected the live sof many including the youth. We all should be united

We all are"EARTHIANS" Planet EARTH is our HOME AND OUR COUNTRY.

"Humanity is our identity and our nationality."

It is very important to note that we should encourage the youth and give them confidence. Youth has the caliber to change the planet. Together let's be united and make our planet better!

●

The Vision of Youth for
Global Politics

Rayan Neja Sidhik
XII-B

Youthplays an important role in the field of politics. The sweat and tears of bothyouth and elderly created histories over centuries.

Nowadays the youth is not getting enough chances to express their political thoughts and views. They must be heard and addressed so that we can channelize it to the betterment of the country. Involving directly or indirectly in the field of politics could make huge difference if the thoughts are young and vibrant. Demonstrations of elections in schools and colleges can give students chances to voice out and understand the epitome of democracy.

Politics should be encouraged among the youths in such a way that the people should feel they are helpful, problem solving and be approached for any social needs. Implication in politics would really help the youth to enhance skills and abilities that are buried in them.

•

The Vision of Youth for
Global Politics

Renate Earnest
VI-B

In today's rapidly evolving world, the significance of science and technology cannot be over stated. It plays an important role in propelling nations towards progress and development. India, with its rich history and diverse population, with no exception. In this article, we will explore the transformative power of science and its multifaceted role in shaping a new country.

Advancing Economic Growth - by fostering innovation, research, and development, India harnessed science to boost its industrial and technological sectors. It has initiatives like "Make in India," the country has witnessed a surge in manufacturing, and job creation. The development of life-saving drugs have improved healthcare outcomes. From the eradication of diseases like polio, COVID-19 etc. India has promoted affordable healthcare services for its citizens. Science has played a major role in addressing public health challenges, such as the COVID-19, through vaccine development .Enhancing Agricultural Productivity, Agriculture forms the backbone of India's economy, to nurture a scientifically inclined society, the Indian government promoted STEM (Science, Technology, Engineering, and

Mathematics) education, and encouraging research and innovation. Science holds the key to India's progress in the 21st century. It empowers the nation to tackle complex challenges, stimulate economic growth, improve healthcare, ensure food security, and foster sustainable development. By harnessing the transformative power of science, India is laying the foundation for a new era of prosperity and innovation. It is poised to become a global leader, making significant contributions to the scientific economy while improving the lives of its citizens.

●

Futuristic India:
Unveiling the True Potential of Science

Rishan Raffic
VIII-C

Science has been a powerful catalyst in ranking India as higher as it is today there by making Indians proud of India. It is the backbone of all the diverse sectors and gives us a scope to look at things in an entirely new way. It is the cornerstone of not only the progress of India, but of the whole world.

The presence of science has saved millions of lives by providing better healthcare. From Aryabhata to the upcoming Chandrayaan-3, all of these space missions would be impossible without a touch of Science. Agriculture, Environmental Sustainability, Technology, AI, IoT, Communication, Economy, Transportation, Infrastructure and Energy, especially Nuclear Power greatly depends on Science. Educational standards have seen drastic improvement with Science being instilled into the minds of children. Without the efforts of great people like C. V. Raman, A. P.J. Abdul Kalam, etc. the humankind would have never experienced the wonders of today. India has showed great development with the country now ranking 3rdin terms of scientific publications and we should continue it. Scienceinvests in the prosperity of our nation more than what we invest in it. Thus, embracing science will turn over a new leaf by empowering India to encounter challenges, seize opportunities, and emerge as a leader in the global arena.

Unlocking India's potential:
The dynamic role of science

Sheiza Shamsuddin
VII-D

India is a democratic country with a unique land of natural vegetation landscape. Before the advent of science, India had many negative aspects, like lack of science institution and methods, caste system and social inequalities, superstitions and beliefs etc. After the advent of science India has witnessed development in engineering , infrastructure, education, space and technology etc.

Present day India has witnessed a rapid integration of science and technology into various aspects driving innovation, society, economic growth, societal development. Here are some achievements of India: Mars Orbiter Mission: In 2014, India launched a mission to Mars , making it the first country to reach Mars. Vaccines: Indian pharmaceutical companies played a crucial role in production of vaccines, including vaccines for polio, measles, and COVID-19. India also developed the most popular innovation AI: Artificial intelligence.

India's development is made possible by science and technology. Science and technology have played a vital role in making India sustainably developed for present and past. India's economical growth is facilitated by it. I believe that with continued scientific innovation and advancing it more, India can develop more than ever.

The Vision of Youth for
Global Politics

Siena Disa Jose

XII-B

Youth- the soul of the society in all aspects including technology, media, science, education etc. Unfortunately, there is no effective participation of youth in global politics. Many policy makers create rules and regulations needed for our communities, countries etc but youth are not given a chance to involve in these matters or to suggest any methods.

Youth is a vast community consisting of strong and weak suggestions, different opinions, creative and extravagant ideas but still are not properly utilized in politics. Young people find it very difficult to recognize themselves as an autonomous community because of inclusive matters, unpaid internships etc. If they are not heard properly, then they move to the streets so that people can heed their concerns. In most of the countries, youth is a community that engages in different sectors including politics. Youth is a heterogeneous group that up bring various issues and concerns that the government can't access to. The global political arena is falling apart and requires a new set of targets, challenges, initiatives etc. The global politics is at stake without new ideas and innovative decisions. It is an important task to bring the youth population into the political platform because the development of the country as well as the people lie in the future generations. It is very visible that the youth or the Gen Z community is not very interested into politics. If the government as well as the nation properly channelize them, within a very short span of time the country would be able to experience the evolution.

●

The Vision Of UAE
for Sustainable Future

Sivani Sunil
X-D

The UAE aims to be one of the main leaders in the area and to create a sustainable environment while protecting the environment and making sure it's not being harmed. Expo 2020 was launched in Dubai as a part of sustainability, opportunity and mobility. It was a six month long program which spreads the different culture of the world. Pavilions of each country was set up. Yet UAE is not stopping there and expanding its vision for UAE's sustainable future

Sheikh Mohammed Bin Rashid Al Maktoum, the ruler of Dubai launched "Green Economy" under the slogan "A green economy for sustainable development". It aims to increase the agriculture, investment and sustainable transport. UAE aims to achieve the sustainable goals which will let the citizens of UAE to access clean water, food, energy and healthy ecosystem. UAE also wants to increase its Gross Domestic Production (GDP) from 1.49 trillion to 3 trillion. The vision for the year 2031 is known worldwide by the name "WE THE UAE 2031". It sets a clear vision for the year 2031.

UAE wants to double its Gross Domestic Production. The UAE citizen are proud of their identity they created which brings a sense of belonging UAE wants to achieve all the aims they set for the future. This makes it clear that UAE has a very clear vision about its future. UAE has been walking through their future with its outstanding ideas. UAE sets a very good example of a sustainable goals.

The vision of UAE
for sustainable future

Snitha Premaraj

X-D

Sustainable development strategies motivate us to practice resource conservation. It maintains equilibrium between our progress and the environment. Meeting both the needs of the current generation and those of the following ones. It is pivotal to avert or stop environmental degradation. The 17 Sustainable Development Goals (SDG) are set to achieve it's aim by the year 2030.

The country UAE wishes to be a global leader in this field, a hub for the export and re-export of green goods and technology, a country that can sustainably develop its economy while preserving the natural resources and environment. The government of the UAE plays a pivotal role in the sustainable development of the country by improving the index of air quality, improving the amount of treated waste among all the waste that is produced in total, enhancing the contribution of clean energy, and improving the index of water scarcity.

The UAE government have introduced a policy or a method to preserve nature by implementing -Green building sustainable building for the

UAE (2010). This is used by the Ministry of infrastructure Development, and is expected to save 10 billion dirhams by the year 2030 and it is predicted to reduce carbon emission by 30%. The UAE is trying to grow trees and plants in this hot region.

The UAE government has introduced cutting edge initiatives. There are many policies and agendas that have been initiated. Vision 2021, Vision 2024, and the Green Agenda UAE 2015-2030 are the key agendas. These three agendas are introduced by HH. Sheikh Mohammed Bin Rashid Al Maktoum. The UAE is trying it's level best to achieve a developed country title and also preserve nature at the same time.

●

The Vision of Youth for Global Politics

Sumaiya

XII-B

The global politics is a world politics which analyses sustainability, equality, justice, and power.

In this modern world, the youth must know about global politics. It deals with citizen rights, legislature, political parties, voting, international relations and government. Usually, a political leader will have experience but in the case of youth they don't have much experience. All they know is about what they have studied about politics in their schooling. If the young leaders are in power, they will be able to bring out new ideas, strategies and opinion which will make a great difference in the country's development. The youth's vision will be progressed towards justice, truthfulness and success. Every democratic government aims for social as well as economic equality which can be achieved by youth. Some of the government in recent times encourages the young leader's power. Every government must take initiative to encourage the youth to learn more about politics and social life during their schooling. The leadership quality of youth will change the development and prosperity of the country. It will bring sustainability and equality.

In my opinion, the youth's power must be encouraged in every country. In india ,the participation of youth in voting is very important, similarly the government can take initiative to make the youth lead the country. The new actions taken by the young leaders will be more effective and efficient.

The Vision of Youth for Global Politics

Surya Sunil Kumar
XI-B

Global politics is the study of the political and economic pattern of a country and its act of securing the nation's goal. Global politics deals with serving justice to all, ensuring citizens' rights, and establishing international relations. Globalization is the major factor that interconnects countries. Though countries have held hands, are they moving towards development or a better future?

The young people are a dominant group among the people. Research has affirmed that the youth in developed countries are excluded from politics, whereas the upcoming minds in underdeveloped countries are either not interested in or do not take part in political activities. The youth in developing countries are exposed to various social and economic issues. Thus, they take part in raising their voice against discrimination, injustice, and inequality. The youth, having the potential to bring about changes, are able to provide a paradigm for an ideal society. The United Nations Democratic Thematic Trust Fund informs public policy making, trains youth to be effective leaders, and improves their participation. With an increase in the rate of education,

youth will begin to develop visions of securing rights for themselves. Their innovative minds can bring about true changes, like preventing conflicts and raising new ideas, to solve a variety of issues. The vision of youth for global politics is the key to shaping the future of where we live.

'Today's youth are tomorrow's leaders, whose collaborative ideas can lift the world to a new standard of living. Not the guns in their hands will develop the nation's minds, but the vision in their minds. The youth should not wait for their vision to become a reality; they have to try to make their ideas of a sustainable and developed world come true. 'The youth' are the new phase of change and development with their vision for the globe.

●

The Vision of Youth for Global Politics

Ummehani Munsi

XII-B

pproximately 78 years ago today, the aftermath of the second world war was showing up, and so, the leaders of the nations gathered to sign an agreement for a more safer and fairer world for everyone. Today, the younger generation and in general the latest generation had seen another historic and devastating moment where the world had fought COVID-19 not long ago. Almost one-third of the world's population are youth whose future will be affected by the on-going geopolitical affairs. It was reported by the UN that two in three countries do not include the young people in poverty education or national plans. The UN system of youth and children has stated that the youth is one of the 'major groups' in the world, yet, they are not given a fair chance to participate and voice out their opinions on global affairs and politics.

In 2019, 1 out of 10 young people had been a victim of not getting proper education and were unemployed. Almost 35% of the world consists of youth between ages 15-24 who face difficulties in getting employed, educated and to start an autonomous life of their own.. The proof given by the UN from a survey conducted amongst youth-led organizations in 45 countries expressed their concerns of the impact on youth's mental health, unemployment, disposable income and education.

The world has been progressing and overcoming the aftermath of COVID-19 and they have set a vision and a mission for youth involvement in politics and global affairs that state, "the primary vision and mission is to acquire public transparency and accountability by enhancing participation of youth in politics to create better solutions and decisions for the crisis found". Many programs and campaigns have been launched and are being acted upon to give chances to children and youth for their involvement in global affairs. One such being ITU's Connect 2030 agenda which calls upon the main priority of connectivity between youth and the digital world. Its goal is to use the latest technology and pros of today's digital world in achieving the SDGs by 2030. Another program launched by the United Nations secretary general is the 'Designers Of Your Own Future', in which youth are invited to contribute their ideas for a better future.

To sum up, the whole point of the involvement of youth in global politics is to birth creative and effective ideas and aims for the future and present to guide us into a peaceful, sustainable and fair world.

Role of Science
in Making New India

Vihaan Hegde
VI-C

Science has played a significant role in the development of any country. India has a variety of scientific resources that aid in making the country better. Humans have used and applied science to increase their quality of living. From the micro to the macro level, research in the field of science has overall enhanced the economic status of India.

India's scientists have made outstanding contributions in the field of science. Medical science has a profound impact on making new India. There used to be a time when deadly epidemics ravaged the world and claimed uncountable lives. Since then, medicines have been invented to cure these diseases. The government of India has made a thoughtful investment in the field of research. Even the agricultural sector has been gifted with tools that reduce the labor and improve their quality of life. On the other hand, the industrial sector has seen a greater yield of finished goods, thereby enhancing India's export business. India has been excelling in space and research due to several inventions which had been made possible by research in science. India is ranked 5th position in the world for scientific research.

Scientific inventions have been employed in various sectors as well. It has helped the country boom economically and will continue to do so. Without using scientific methods and techniques we would not have been able to develop the country to the extent it has developed today.

●

The Vision of Youth for Global Politics

Waaeeza Usman
XII-D

The UN has stated that around one-third of the world's population is below the age of eighteen. Young people's voice to create an impactful and sustainable global institution is called for. Yet the modern youth is doing anything but that in all practicality. Now a question may arise, what is youth politics? Youth politics encompasses a policy where young leaders take part in the political decisions and processes including youth organizations and lifestyle. In countries like Uganda and Somalia about two-thirds of the population is below the age of twenty-five. Yet this group remains uninvolved in the decision making process of the government and are frustrated because of the lack of vision for youth in global politics.

But there is a solution: Generation Democracy. Generation Democracy offers a platform for young leaders to discuss opportunities and strategies for mobilizing their peers so that they can regulate and advance youth participation in global politics. Generation Democracy was launched by the International Republican Institute (IRI) in 2015 making a global network of young leaders across 70 countries. The

second Generation Democracy Global Summit was conducted in May 2018, bringing about 40 young leaders across 35 countries.

One key output of the Global Summit was Generation Democracy Vision 2020. The vision was formulated through a process where young delegates participated and came up with pathways to keep the momentum of the conference.

Lipi Mehta, a young social activist and leader expressed her views about global politics and youth participation by saying: "In India, even now everyone goes off to protest on the streets because we feel that's the only way we'll be heard. By 2020, I hope that we could not just be a part of protests but also a part of the policy." By introducing Generation Democracy, the lack of youth participation in global politics won't be completely avoided but at the least, reduced bit by bit.

It's about time now for the youth to finally be serious and take actions accordingly for their voices to be heard and Generation Democracy is going to help people achieve that exactly. It's now or never.

●